My
Time
with
Papa

by

Shauntae Spaulding

Tellwell Talent
www.tellwell.ca

ISBN
978-0-2288-3073-3 (Hardcover)
978-0-2288-3072-6 (Paperback)

FOR: KARTER LYNN

DEDICATED TO: BRYAN

When I was playing with my toys, Mama got a call. She looked really sad as she started to fall. I asked her what was wrong as I wiped her face. She said, "Papa has gone with the angels to another place."

I asked, "Can I go too?" and she said,

"No, it's not time for you."

I said, "I will miss him and all the fun things we used to do."

"Don't worry," she said, "he'll still be part of the team. When you close your eyes and think of Papa, he'll be alive in your dreams."

I close my eyes and I see Papa waiting for me. He holds out his strong hand as he motions for us to leave.

He takes me to our favorite ice cream shop and says I can have not one scoop but three! Then we head to the pet store to get a new kitty and I name her Bumblebee.

Papa likes to ride bikes but not the one I can ride. I get on my tricycle and I am ready to drive!

Papa loves to play softball and he teaches me how to catch. I am not very good at it yet so the ball rolls down in the ditch.

Next, we go swimming which is my favorite thing to do! Papa lifts me up in the air like an airplane and I go zoom, zoom, zoom!

Pool time is done and it's time to play. Riding on Papa's big back is so much fun, I could do it all day!

Now it's time for dress up and I search everywhere for my kitty dress. Papa just watches with a smile on his face as I make a huge mess.

It's time for cleanup and I put all my stuff away. Then Papa says, "Playtime is over and I can no longer stay."

He gives me a kiss and says he had fun and not to forget him while he is gone. Then with a big hug he says, "As long as you remember me when you close your eyes, we will continue on."

I opened my eyes to see Mama smiling at me. She asked if I had fun while I played with Papa in my dreams.

I nodded my head and gave her a kiss. Papa, I love him, and he will always be missed.

ABOUT THE AUTHOR

Shauntae Spaulding currently resides in the San Fernando Valley with her son. She enjoys reading, watching movies, and spending time outdoors. She wrote this book after the death of her stepfather and dedicates it to her niece, Karter Lynn. She hopes that you will find a sense of peace and happiness after losing a loved one and know that the memories you shared will always remain.